Diego's Serenade of Thoughts: Poetry Unchained

Poetry's Flight through Diego's Mind

Diego Hernandez

Contents

Dedication

This book is dedicated to God, my family, Mr. Jones, and Mr. Aviles.

Acknowledgments

Recently, Diego Hernandez won an award from the Young Writers Association and has been elected for publication in a magazine with other poets around the country. Diego Hernandez currently holds three honor roll awards, which are school awards for students with all A's and Bs in their grades.

About the Author

In a little island between three oceans named Cuba, more specifically La Habana Cuba, in a small town named 'Playa". Diego Hernandez Moreno was born on July 7, 2007, in the year 2007. He grew up in an honest and hardworking family with "privileges". His lovely dad was a security guard for the United States embassy in Cuba, and my mom is a hairdresser with her own place. Growing up, Diego found a passion for helping people, as his first dream was to become a lawyer. Later on, he fell in love with history and decided to write about it, and later on, he started writing poetry. At the age of 16, he decided to make a difference in his life and decided to grow up and publish a book about his poems, showing his ideals. Diego's favorite movie is "The Patriot" , his favorite song is 'Nessun Dorma" by Luciano Pavarotti, or "Big P", and his favorite book is "Ten Caesars ". Diego hopes that you find this book interesting and that you find a lovely trajectory as you dive inside his mind.

1. Growing; Destroying

Once upon a time

    There were only trees.

    Trees flirting with their leaves.

    Leaves flirting with the dirt.

    Animals living peacefully on Earth.

    Humans growing, trees getting the damages.

    Animals getting extinguished because of us.

Humans are monsters whose food is money.

Money is a sword that cuts through the hearts of animals.

Animals are terrified of us and are crying for their pears.

    While we are just eating meat

    Eating meat while drinking Vodka

The Earth is no longer safe in our hands.

    With us

Dear Lion, please forgive me.

    Dear Deer, please don't cry.

Please don't cry because I will fight.

    Oh, please forgive me!

    Not all of us are monsters.

    Who betrays their own kind?

    Their own kind

Oh, dear God!

Oh, dear God!

Please tell me how you are going to survive.

    Survive seeing us without crying.

    Without being regretful

    Without wanting the end

Imagine all the people.

    Letting living things live.

    A world without wars

    Without racism

    Don't matter your religion.

    Or your color

    We must stop this genocide.

    Does it for our children?

    Does it for humanity?

2.   Dear Cauley

Dear Cauley, it's been a day since I left your leave.
Your beautiful leaves, where you can smell peace.
Your beautiful, old-fashioned ways make me seem old.
Old as your books, new as your employees who see gold.
As gold as the peacocks who were near my arm, those
moments were cold.

In the fountain, I was standing where my brother was
holding my hand.

Taking pictures in Cauley Square to make my children
understand.

Everything was going swimmingly until the rain and
exhaustion set in.

We entered a Renaissance Museum to see a copy of the
Sistine Chapel,
whose commanding

Command our eyes to look back in time to the rebirth of art.
That everyone was beginning to understand.
Understand what today's people don't care about.
They don't feel pain, Cauley. I give you my hand.

Salchipapa, Salchipapa was in my happy mouth who felt those wonderful times.

I see it as a crime that sometimes people respond "all of the above."
About what foods they have tried.
There were peacocks and peacocks everywhere,
and the whole family was there to be a model in my photos,
where you can apply.

Where is the bridge where I will be stationed as a Spanish general?
conquering the land and the sky
I went fast towards those high stairs to see the Museum of Art,
where I saw a Cuban guy, dry leaves flying high by my eye,
and asking,
"Why is this place like Dubai?"

3.   Fingers Moving

The words that describe your ideas

Someone's eyes are displaying your thoughts.

Making a positive difference in people's live

You are experiencing agony in your daily life.

Nevertheless, your medicine is millennial.

"Poetry" is the name of your pain medicine.

Your day may be terrible.

Yet, poetry makes you appear charming.

Poetry is a part of your life; even if you never use it, you are a poet.

Because you rhyme daily.

Every day of your life, you utter insightful things.

Using metaphorical language to avoid speaking lite.

For hundreds or thousands of years

Poetry has been the world's language.

Our language has become clever since Shakespeare.

Smart as Einstein, as astute as Hawking.

Since we used pens and ink to write,

Using a writing machine to write

To make Microsoft our way of life

Even nonliving stories being read about them are potent in our world.

Poetry on natural catastrophes

We live in a technological world that is influenced by poetry.

4.   Missing my mysterious memory.

It was just dark.

When the clowns told us never to come back

Never come back where my DNA belongs.

It was just dark to start a new life.

New friends and new discoveries

Even if my dad was 54 in this place, he was 5.

My mysterious memory

Mysterious because I forgot.

Forgot to never forget.

Never forget new memories.

And hold in a special jar the bad old ones.

And in my heart, the good old ones

Miss my country

But never the ones who ruled it.

5.   The wrong side of the coin

A sailor is trying to find land.

He can't see; there is fog all over the boat.

He was with his son, a young writer.

He was writing a new poem; it might be his last one.

The helmsman is trying to guide them with his impacting light.

But they still can't see; there is fog all over the skies.

Father has taught his young boy how to sail.

How to be a man in this world

How to never have problems in your life

But that ongoing training can't be finished if they vanish in the fog.

The helmsman is trying to save the sailors.

She realizes that there is no chance of surviving but rather a chance of death.

She decides to call her friend Tommy "a white captain with a Titanic."

The white captain and his black slaves are trying to find the forgotten two.

In these quicksilver waters, it is difficult to find a small boat.

It is difficult to find the forgotten two.

In 1910, it was a time of war; it was impossible not to know what was going to happen.

What's going to happen if you are black and others are
white?
When they found the father and his son,
Dying from wounds, dying drowning
When the captain saw their color
He decides to scream "nothing" to the family's nephews.

Later, when the moon settles,
Their bodies were found.
I found them as cold as ice.
Found their eyes in a state of depression.
Dye because of a natural choice
a natural choice that no one can make.
And that was that they were born on the wrong timeline, on
the wrong side of the coin.

6.   Suicide Media

Vanish in the wind, crying; vanish in the fog.

Flowers withered, and parents had questions.

Imagine all the pain the world is feeling.

Imagine all the troubles and tears these media have caused.

Whether for good or bad, imagine the agony of those withered flowers.

The sky is blue, but on the ground, there are tears.

There is dirt in the environment and withered flowers.

People might say that I'm a dreamer.

But there are many dreamers like me.

Who wants a better world with no types of bullying?

Pigeons deliver a sorrowful message.

The paper holding those sorrowful letters.

Trees being cut and pigeons slaves for sadness.

Cyberbullying is a lethal weapon.

Depression is happening around the globe.

Imagine all the people sharing a peaceful world.

A world where pigeons and trees don't die.

People are gathering in black clothes and with a tissue in hand.

Because of the pain you have caused, oh, human, what have you done?

Depression is happening around the world.

7. Love for Scandinavia

Nine Realms is another Davinci art.

Discipline and creatures in battles

Just because it's a sign of respect.

Respect for the God of wisdom

They used to do it for the All-Father.

Fighting each battle like it might be their last one.

fighting each day of their lives for respect, for their families

For the All-Father

They say that Ragnarök was their apocalypse.

But the real apocalypse for a Viking life is to be useless.

Useless for the nine realms, useless to your family

Losing their sense of living

Odin is no longer with them.

Asgard, Alfheim, Niavellir, Midgard

Jotunheim, Vaanaheim, Niflheim, Muspelheim, and Hel

Men being men, fighting for their beliefs, family, and
reputation.

Killing anyone who disrespects their family or them.

8.   For the Future

What shoes shall we wear?
Standing naked in a throng of poverty and brokenness,
More than eight billion people have died as a result of conflicts.

Today is meaningless to the clock ahead of us.
Because there is no money, the clock may vanish.
There is no money, no weapons, and no individuals who are psychologically alive.

Simply because of conflicts in the name of liberty.
Putting those in charge of our lives
 who just care about having greener in their slacks.

Where mankind will be in 20 years
"Learning uncensored allows people to see what is censored."
We face mental fights every day of our lives.
Fill the void with implanted mediocrity.

9.   Spring Horror

From Sumerians to this age group

On hand, live reports

I'll tell you some petrifying tales.

And in every one of those tales, broach the same beast.

He appears at a camp.

Eating with happiness

in agony, laughing.

clearing up his mess

Run into an elongated bath.

When the blood drains from his body

The Spring Monster has awakened.

Everyone was scared.

Spring

Spring is deadly.

10.   Hold Tight; Its Coming

Years have passed, and you're still waiting.

You are creating, hating, awaiting.

For the future, relating all possible outcomes.

A new era is upon us, so hold on tight, black panther.

It's on its way to your people; wait for your response.

Your answer to your cancer: Doesn't let them beat you.

You are a black panther, not a coward. Stand up and show them
their screws. Creating, hating, awaiting

For the future, relating all possible outcomes.

A new era is upon us, so hold on tight, black panther.

It's on its way to your people; wait for your response.

Your answer to your cancer: Doesn't let them beat you.

You are a black panther, not a coward. Stand up and show them
their screws.

Hold tight; it's coming.

Becoming, running, looking stunning

Remember, black panther it's coming.

Your prayers have been answered, Alexander.

Your people will finally see the light at the end of the tunnel.

All your people struggled through this year.

Are finally beginning to show up.

Years have passed, and you're still waiting.

You are creating, hating, awaiting.

Hello, Hello

Respect is the universal language of the world.

But I suppose Loki was unaware.

Patience opens doors, so don't close them.

Watching funny stuff is what they choose for us.

When the whole world is missing this universal war

Respect is the universal language of the world.

You are a black panther, not a coward.

Stand up and show them their screws.

Hold tight, it's coming.

Becoming, running, looking stunning

Years have passed, and you're still waiting.

You are creating, hating, awaiting.

Hold tight, my friend.

My friend of all these years

In the good and bad

You were always by my side.

Thank you! Thank you, my friend.

For holding tight.

Wakanda Forever

Forever, together

And together forever

Wakanda, Wakanda

Always unite.

Not letting anyone touch my eyes.

11. Dear God

God, I am so grateful.

I'm grateful that you let me put on shoes.

Please help those who ask for it.

They don't wait well.

They are not feeling well.

Having a depressed mood.

God, I am so grateful.

I appreciate you giving my family permission to buy groceries.

Assist the people who need it.

Perseverance is challenging in our world.

Those in need have references.

Please, God, help those who are in need.

They are in dire need of a charismatic leader,

who can guide them to success.

Peace be with you, last glory.

I really thank God for everything.

Rest in ultimate splendor.

I sincerely appreciate everything I have, God.

Please assist those who lack my rights as well.

12.   The Heart of the Guitar

Greetings, fairly, I shall say hello.

With a grenade in my shady heart about to detonate

not in a rose garden but in an empty, dark room.

Since my human bought me, my strings won't move.

I feel abandoned.

Greetings to the villain who never dared.

It's true that I'm new.

It's terrible that I'm inferior to others.

My strings should be food for people's ears.

Not covered in mud.

Guitars have hearts.

"Hearts with feelings"

Guitars should be played.

Not being forgotten in the corner

Thank you for messing up my career.

Rather, I shall say life.

13.   Baby Bring Back the Beers

There is an empyrean.

That drops tears.

Shares it with the bears.

In South America, giving prayers

Every day of our lives

Our hands are being warmed by the sun.

Antarctica is melting because of us.

Trees are dying because of us.

Welkin visually examining our pros and cons.

But, even if my ocular perceivers remain motionless,

I'm probing for a fighting partner.

In any place, it doesn't matter; it's time.

If it's proximate to the Atlantic or Pacific

I will still be waiting.

Waiting for the firmament, sun,

and trees to go red.

Not because of a threat,

but because of profound appreciation.

Baby, bring the potations!

We're looking forward to a good time.

a good time because I have you between my rhymes

I recall my malefactions from time to time.

The malefactions that haunt me every day of my life

Those malefactions, I should describe in five words.
"I will always profoundly relish you."
Firmament, Sun, and Tree
Please come down to me
Mermaids appearing, singing.
Waiting for the ceremony that we are bringing.
The crabs designing.
And Pandas preparing the pabulum.
Dolphins take care of security.
It will be wondrous tonight with our maturity.
With you holding my hand

Baby, bring the potations!
We're looking forward to a good time.
a good time because I have you between my rhymes
I recall my malefactions from time to time.
The malefactions that haunt me every day of my life

People from all over the world
Africa, Europe, and from the Americas
Coming to visually perceive the Earth's ceremony.
We are going to a party.
We are going to party astutely.
All night long

All night long, we are going to party.

Going to party vigorously

I'm going to party vigorously with you right contiguous to me.

Holding my nervous hand.

And saying, "I dote on you."

14.   Son, carry on

Hello, son.

Welcome to this world. Our family's reputation is now in your

capable hands.

I should teach you how to gamble for our sake.

How to Keep Your Nobility

People with intellectual spirits live under the ozone layer.

The calix of life is rushing, and every grain of sand must be

used.

You must keep our secrets.

Keep going with our business.

Carry on, dear son.

Continue my legacy.

Continue with your life.

Leave me alone.

Because I'm nothing more than a candle in the wind.

15.   While the story change, the goal remains

Folktales that scare young children

showing smiles

Reminding adults of what they experienced. Despite story changes, the objective remains.

Reality is altered by holiness.

The Vikings' tales differ, but their goal is always the same:

changing literature to reflect their ideals.

constructing a bubble full of lies

Making inaccurate assumptions that will influence future generations.

16.   Anxiety for Traveling

Italy and Greece

France and Spain

Iceland and Norway

What amazing nature!

With its culture, Spain

France's urban landscape, the natural beauty of Norway, and

Iceland

Wow, what an amazing universe!

Anxiety related to travel.

It hurts my pocketbook.

I daydream of accomplishing my goals one day.

Want to experience Spain's departure? Feel Greek

architecture.

What a wonderful world we live in!

Take me, Mom, Dad, and brother, please.

Show me the real ham, please.

Where the Vikings used to battle for their lives, the truth

baguette dwells.

Travel-related anxiety is increasing.

As a result of climate change.

Reducing the likelihood that my world's rivers will be able

to preserve the weather.

He has leaves.

What a beautiful planet we live on!

23

17.   Pigeons Meeting

In the trees, we assemble.

The trees make us live.

Without them, we disappear.

Seeing my family fly

Up to the top of the home

Only a few of us have lived.

We are assembling in order to radiate.

Owls are arriving.

Run

Cutting my home

Fellow animals that live in trees

Extinguish

Extinguish

Is there now a thirst?

Hero may have called you, but the same as clashing.

18.   Creation

We are stepping into a gigantic body.

Hair is the tree.

Blood, we swim.

Bones are walls; security for all.

Death of a Frozen Giant

Shaping began

All fathers with their families

Fighting and creating

The eyes as they are today.

19.   Beauty of Birds

Flying at the top of the tree
with a smile full of life
with a heart full of tales
Living in manumission

Every animal should follow.
Bird's shines
We destroy.
Flying at the top of the tree

Living in manumission
with a smile full of life
Putting a shield on their race
Not letting extinction show happiness.

Lions are smart, not strong.
Strong are the elephants.
Fast are the Panthers.
Never did they know that the lion was the King.

20. Night without moon

Hearing the wolf's howl

Darkening the world

Seeing no signs of life

No life without the moon.

Don't smack me in the eyes; I'm afraid of light.

Let me recline with my owls at night.

21. May brightness

Stars aligning

Comets arriving

Galaxy waiting

Shiny May

Shiny month

Party like twenty

In the tenth.

22.   Heredity

Within every one of us

There is still life.

There are clocks that stop working.

We notice that small hand when we see it.

Warm and little hand

The time is 29:29.

That small hand is no more.

A long-lasting hand yields a little hand.

A new warm hand is being extended.

Helping warm to become chilly.

Giving our children safety

Attempting to end our life.

As a result, they can run.

Run, run, baby.

And don't turn around.

Oh, sweet child.

Don't turn around.

Because you might never smile if you look around.

23.   Human, then Ghost

Hello, fellow citizens.
You've joined the cast.
Cast that burden on the writers.
Writers of a dark script

Explosion; Explosion
Can't run or touch.
Bye, fellow Ghost.
We prize you.

Goals shattered.
Can't run or touch.
Now, you are stuck in a new world.
New life

Just for shattered goals
Money is not luminary.
If you have no health, no legs, or no arms,
a world of cowards, an illegal world

24.   Garden smell

Sunlight intensity

With a point, the world moves.

A new day has arrived.

Happy fresh, bright day!

Considering the next 20 years

My veins are filled with passion.

Poetry smells like a garden.

My other side is poetry.

Something appears ludicrous in poetry.

The garden requires upkeep.

The same as poetry

One more night, sweet word

Do you sense love?

Love runs through your veins.

Poetry is the name given to love.

25. A world of purple flowers

Come in, children.
To meet my world
A world of purple flowers
Where fun is the rule.

26. Destiny

There's a bird there.
Flying through the night
awaiting a change.
Seeing individuals in embarrassment
Seeing ourselves imprisoned
Lock till we get together.
Your eyes are the sky.
Your smile on the red carpet
Makes me seem like a fool.
Lady, we belong together.
Together forever
My beautiful star in the sky.

27.   Waiting for merriment

Sun settles
Going to bed
Disposed to see the sun again.
Sour over the night

Pop or rock?
Rap or disco?
Sun settles
Music is water to me.

Music is a treasure.
My little precious treasure
Love for music
Another day, same love

Long eyes
Powerful eyes
Air through my face
Music is just another time in my heart.

28. Twenty steps into the future

Dead air

Flowing through my veins

Honoring light and night

Moving on and seeing myself

My body on the highest mountain

Grabbing hands with my life

Saying into her eyes

Sorry, my son.

Sadly, white will shine.

God help me.

Twenty steps forward

Seeing every step dark

Seeing dead friends

Dead air

Around me.

29.   Raining in red

More than 200
Less than 300
Days raining
World without light

Big eyes
See everything.
White smashing black
God left the world.

Sky seeing blood.
Sun withdrawing
Year after year
Sovereignty feeling isolated.

Wind facing dead.
Hold my son.
Sovereignty left us.
Black child punished.

Wars for "authority"
For red money
Raining in red.

30.   Back in 7

World without cream
Without happiness
Can't be called a world.
Back in 7

Back in 7
The world wasn't the same.
Sunny sky
Great old days

Spending time with family
Ignoring the evil world
Putting my body in the white snow
My face in the cold waters

Back in 7
Years for men have passed quickly.
Hand holding a soda.
Night with light

Back in 7, traveling.
Back in seven, eyes were showing gold.
Dark times today; happy the ones before
Living life like an addict, an addict of happiness.

31.   The Lady in the Tree

The Amorist Dark Tree
In which a girl resides
The Aphonic Girl
Arcane girl

Inside, there's a refrain.
Asunder by her own race
Eyes reflect life.
Night; light handing the wine

Arcane girl fighting to survive.
In the shady days of life.

32. World

Without family, is a world with no eyes.

33. Honor

Fighting to guard us
Air holding isolation
Eyes have not seen life.
No sign of life

Dark white
No sign of life
Water in red
Days pass by.

Soldiers welcome back
To your lost world
Sun saying thank you
Thank you for saving our world.

Welcome back, soldier.
Gratitude for your kindness.

34.   Seeing without Eyes

Out of the world
World without clocks
World without problems
Everything is gold

Walking on heaven
Seeing ourselves in white
Not worrying about time
Seeing our world collapse

Laughing at death
Seeing ourselves rising
with the galaxies
Help me, father

Eating the never-try food
Bodies resting
Resting with our savior
Rising in the galaxies

Water flowing
Inside of us.

35. False Faith

Just a man in green
Men with swords
The enemy with sticks
Unfair fight

Unfair fight, the one we are seeing
No scouts for the enemy
Blind and deaf enemy
Receiving what is told

Time is their fortress.
Their blood is their puppet.
Shall we fight, or shall we calm?
Why?

Dying of hunger
No availability of clean water
Night is light.
Eyes are dark.

36.   In the Tapestry of Tomorrow

The brightly embroidered tapestry of the future
advancing threads yearning towards the light,
Unknown future events still lie ahead.
A tale of marvels that has yet to be told.

Glass cityscapes that reach the sky

Where innovation and aspirations never die,

Airborne electric currents hum,

Everywhere, there is a symphony of technology,

AI and robots go hand in hand.

They dance throughout the countryside with people.

A synthesis of ideas, a cosmic mixture,

We transcend in this brave new world.

Science and nature coexist in harmony.

Taking a caring step toward healing the Earth

Solar Power; a beautiful song

A pledge to turn back the erroneous directions we've gone.
We set our sights on the universe as we explore.

distant lights on planets and stars,

We are not in the embrace of the cosmos.

37.   Two-Hearths

Two hearts linked in a gentle embrace among fields of golden sunlight's splendor

Love's charming song, with such a lovely tune,

I'll be forever entwined in your arms.

Your eyes, like brightly gleaming stars,

The unending fantasy of love

My heart beats faster with each glance.

Lost in the depths of true love's light

A delicate touch, a kind phrase,

I'm forever aroused by your love's ocean.

We'll find our way through storms and quiet.

Our love will never waver as long as we are together.

In the echoes of laughter and grief,

Nothing compares to the strength of their friendship.

You are my love, the genuine rhyme of my heart.

Forever dancing over time's sands.

So, come what may, let us embrace each passing day.
In the wonderful rhythm of love.
Our souls will continue to rhyme in perpetuity.
For all time, two hearts are joined.

38. Halls of Study

Minds trapped in study halls
The system's bounds, a broken route,
Thoughts were caged like birds and forbidden to fly.
Creativity slips into obscurity.

Standardized assessments, similar to hard walls,
As it spreads, it limits its potential.
Individual stars, hidden by darkness,
Shadows are uniform, and there is a lack of light.

Teachers, who were once stars in the eyes of their pupils,
Now lost in commands and hushed screams,
They strive to extinguish the flame of curiosity.
We all suffocate in inflexible boxes.

Let us break these bonds and enjoy the arts.
Unchain your brains, and let greatness begin.
Education thrives when it is unrestricted.
There is a universe of wonders to be discovered.

39. Society

In the middle of the city's bright glare,

We carry a tangled web of miseries,

and society's maladies interpose.

Like vipers beneath the bloom.

Lost souls float away like unbound ships.

Dreams are battered in shallow waters.

Their laughter is masked by a quiet scream.

A river flows in the opposite direction as the stream.

We fumble through life's tangled mass,

our souls knotted with fruitless anxieties,

while shadows dance on cracked glass.

A maze of uncertainties and sorrow.

"The world is too much for us," he said.

A poet's truth, always free,

However, contemporary life, like a sterile prison,

dims nature's radiance with suppressed wrath.

As if they were puppets in a huge farce,

We perform our parts, but the obligations are never paid.

We watch the performance in Plato's cave,

unaware of Reality's depths.

But there is still a gleam in the gloom.

A glimmer of hope, a chance to fight

Transformation begins with unchained hearts.

A regained mental revolution.

So, let us repair the rifts in society.

We sway with empathy and affection.

Seek the light from above in the midst of the darkness.

And mend the hurting lover's scars.

40. Into my Peaceful World

Nations weaved together like a dream,
governments as one, hand in hand,
creating a tapestry throughout the country in a world where
unity reigns supreme.

Borders have been removed, and divisions have been
reversed.
A melody of peace that has just recently begun,
Flags of peace float in the air.
As nations unify and warfare subsides.

No more conflicts, no more weapons.
Only knowledge and compassion are shown.
Cultural riches spread far and wide.
In this world, hearts and minds collide.

Languages mingle, and diversity is embraced.
From East to West and North to South,
We rely on a worldwide family.
Love's unending darkness on a unified planet

Children grow up in a delightful environment.
Their future was bathed in a golden light.
Education flourishes; knowledge soars, guided by wisdom
so pure and bright.
Hunger and poverty are becoming relics of the past.

As nations unify, no one is left out.

A world in which resources are shared by everyone.

We stand tall on this shared path.

Nature thrives in this period of agreement; oceans are preserved,

Trees are cherished, and a sustainable planet is created for future generations.

Every daughter and son will inherit a heritage of harmony.

Let us imagine a world of grace, where disputes fade away, leaving no trace, governments unite, and hearts are entwined.

We discover a world of peace together.

41. General

The sun's wisdom unfurled,
Strategies like pearls, a swirl,
The warrior's mind twirls.

42.   Dear Nature

Amidst the wild, where rivers softly croon,

Nature's canvas painted, lush and grand,

A symphony of life beneath the moon

The forest stands like an ancient sentinel.

Its leafy arms embrace the earth's demands.

Amidst the wild, where rivers softly croon.

Mountains rise, their peaks like crowns of old,

In majesty, they touch the heavens' hand,

A symphony of life beneath the moon

The meadows dance, their colors a festoon,

where blossoms bloom like dreams upon the land

amidst the wild, where rivers softly croon.

The ocean's voice is a constant, soothing tune.

Its waves are a testament to time's own sand.

A symphony of life beneath the moon

Through the seasons' wheel, where stories are strewn,

Nature weaves its tales into a wondrous strand.

Amidst the wild, where rivers softly croon,

A symphony of life beneath the moon

43.   All-Father

In ancient lands where stars would sing,

A tale of hope began to cling,

A baby born beneath the sky,

A manger's warmth, a star on high

A shepherd's heart, a guiding light,

As wise men followed through the night,

A humble birth, a world reborn,

In Bethlehem, a Savior's dawn

He walked on water, calmed the sea,

With mustard seeds, faith's mystery,

He healed the sick and gave them sight.

A touch that filled the darkest night

As wheat and fish multiplied,

His love embraced both low and high.

A shepherd's care for wayward sheep,

A love so wide, so vast, so deep

A parable, a tale, a song,

In tales of grace, the weak grew strong.

A fig tree's lesson, lilies dressed,

His teachings were simple, and his heart was impressed.

With bread and wine, a sacred feast,

His body was broken, love was released,
A covenant of grace untold
In wine transformed, a truth of old

Yet shadows began to loom,
A cross awaited certain doom,
He bore the weight of sin's cruel sting.
A crown of thorns, a sacrifice, King

Upon the hill, a cross of pain,
Redemption's purpose is not in vain,
He cried, forgave, and conquered death.
With his dying breath, he gave us breath.

But from the tomb, he rose anew.
In victory, a promise comes true,
A stone rolled back, an empty grave,
He came to heal, seek, and save.

And through the ages, faith takes flight.
In Christ's embrace, we find our light.
His love is like rivers, deep and wide.
Flows through our hearts like a constant tide.

So let the story ever soar.
In every heart, forevermore,
A tale of grace and divine love
In every soul, a sacred sign

44. Tomorrow

Crystal dreams unfold,

Tomorrow's tears now sown,

Hope blooms through sorrow.

45. Automated Future

An electronic mind takes flight in the dance of circuits.

A code symphony, the glimmer of the future,

Whereas mind and silicon meet in sight,

awakening a universe that was previously considered unreal.

Observe the emergence of fake elegance.

An intricate web of algorithms,

It is put where it belongs in every world,

when the first advancement tendrils emerge.

However, we consider what fates lie ahead.

When metal brains reflect human cognition,

Will development lead or sway the strands of fate?

Embraced by silicon, are we trapped?

When futures combine, a partnership is created.

A new world will be known when we are bonded together.

46.   Trusting a Dream

In the ivory towers of intellect, we dwell.

Like ancient Rome, our tales of wisdom swell.

Through corridors of thought

We strive, Seeking truths, like Caesar's conquest, far and

wide.

As scholars lost in Plato's sacred cave,

We quest for knowledge—knowledge to engrave.

Our minds, like sculptors, chisel, shape, and refine

To build the grandeur of divine life.

The tapestry of life is a web we weave

With threads of hope and passion to believe.

Just as Rome's mighty empire rose and fell,

so do moments in our mortal shell.

As Caesar dared the Rubicon to be crossed,

We brave our challenges and our paths emboss.

In every lecture hall is a Senate space,

Where ideas duel and minds embrace.

Through Socratic debates, we learn to see

The truths that bind our human tapestry

Like Virgil's verses, guiding lost souls through

We chart our courses and dreams anew.

Oh, Horace's Ode to Life's swift
Fleeting art Reminds us that each day is but a part
So seize the moments,
Carpet Diem's call, For a time, relentless, waits not for us all.

In libraries, where echoes of the past
Resound like echoes in a marble vast
We grasp the shoulders of giants there
To reach for the stars and breathe rarefied air.

But like the Colosseum's crumbling grace,
Our intellects, too, must find their place
In cycles of creation, growth, and decline,
We, too, must strive, climb, and shine.

For as Rome's glories waned in history's pen,
We pen our futures, writing with the yen,
To leave our mark, our legacy, our rhyme,
In annals vast, in the grand march of time.

So, let us learn from Rome's majestic reign.
And from its fall, let wisdom's seed remain
Embrace each challenge and seize each precious day,
Like Caesar's Rome, in our own destined way.

47.   World of Ideals

Power remains hot.
The truth remains cold.
World of educated fellows
Shall say world of seekers

Seekers who see a dream
The dream of new ideas
Filling the antiquated can
A dream more powerful than an empire

More powerful than themselves
Seeking independence
Of a divided nation
"New ideas are everywhere, but not the appropriate few."

48.   Endless Love

My heart's song, Alyssa
The light of love is in your eyes.
Stars lust after your elegance.

Moonlight leaves a trace in your grin.

leaking cosmic espionage,

Your chuckle is sincere.

In the warmth of the sun and your touch,

Time stands still in your cozy grip.

The melody of love shines.

Under the velvet dreamscape of the night,

Alyssa, the scene in my heart

You are my never-ending rhyme.

49. Feelings Towards Writing

Like rivers of yearning, ink flows.

A fierce fire spreads across the page

as words blossom like spring blossoms.

A kaleidoscope of feelings they evoke.

Each metaphor is a dove whispered.

Personification gives the wind voices,

As the passionate singing fires of exaggeration

You're a moonlight kiss, writing.

A melody of blissful desire

Your poetry, lovely wine strands,

enthrall like heavenly love.

Landscapes are painted in the imagination via imagery.

Mountains of ideas, undefined valleys,

Rhymes cascade boldly like cascades.

Every sentence tells a love story.

We investigate using pens and keyboards.

worlds within, and a lot more,
fingers covered in ink, hearts unbound

My dear writing, you make me whole.

50.   A Little History of My Roots

Born without world

Hidden Place

Of hope and hankering

Supporting ourselves

While surviving.